ROOM IN ROME

JORGE EDUARDO EIELSON

TRANSLATED FROM THE
SPANISH BY DAVID SHOOK

CARDBOARD HOUSE PRESS
www.cardboardhousepress.org
cardboardhousepress@gmail.com

HABITACIÓN EN ROMA / ROOM IN ROME
Copyright © 2019 Martha Canfield
Translation © 2019 David Shook
"Vivir es una obra maestra" © 2008 Mario Vargas Llosa
Author photograph © Centro Studi Jorge Eielson
"Bandiere," by Jorge Eduardo Eielson, photograph © Karina Valcárcel
Designed by Mutandis

First Edition, 2019
Printed in the United States of America
ISBN 978-1-945720-18-5
Distributed by Small Press Distribution

TO LIVE IS A MASTERPIECE

Mario Vargas Llosa

Jorge Eduardo Eielson (1924-2006) belonged to the so-called "Generation of 1950," which broke decisively with the limitations of regionalism and played a part in ushering Peruvian poetry into modernity. In this undertaking, the group followed the examples of some of its most illustrious predecessors: José María Eguren, César Vallejo, Martín Adán, César Moro, and Emilio Adolfo Westphalen.

Among the poets of the "Generation of 1950," whose members included Javier Sologuren, Sebastián Salazar Bondy, Blanca Varela, Raúl Deustua, and Carlos Germán Belli, Eielson was one of the most precocious and unique. He was a passionate reader of the classics, the Greeks, the writers of the Spanish Golden Age, and of French poetry, Rilke, and the Surrealists, and his first publications —after his early *Reinos* (1945)— reveal a poet with a sensual, exalted, highly personal voice aspiring to make the greatest cultural traditions of the West his own. Two years earlier, in 1943, he had written a beautiful, visionary transfiguration of *La Chanson de Roland* (*The Song of Roland*), a poem in prose that, in its evocation of the celebrated heroism at Roncevaux, flows like a river of bold and unpredictable images and verbal beauty. Antigone, Ajax, and Don Quixote prompt further lyrical explorations through which the young creator displays the universality of his calling through agile use of the classics as a springboard to develop his own lyric personality. By 1949, when Eielson left for Europe, where he would spend the rest of his life, he had already become a seasoned poet with a singular voice, and, culturally speaking, a citizen of the world.

Eielson would never abandon his position as an artist without boundaries—neither geographical nor cultural—and would maintain a fierce, open, and curious spirit throughout his life. Never content to focus on one art form at a time, this spirit would inspire him to jump from poetry to painting, to theatre, to novels, to productions (he called them "performances" and "actions"), to installations, and even to the circus (he told Martha Canfield with the utmost seriousness that he only considered himself an "acrobat" and a "clown"). He was interested in everything: archeology, science, religion, and above all, from the end of the 1950s on, in Zen Buddhism. He participated in some way in every intellectual and artistic trend of post-war Europe, though he never belonged to any school or group and always defended his independence and solitude. Even at the peak of his public visibility, when he "placed" invisible poems in spaceships or on famous public monuments, he kept a cautious, secret distance from what he was doing. Unlike other contemporary artists who often resorted to buffoonery for self-promotion, Eielson demonstrated a life-long, Olympic indifference to success and a rigorous seriousness in all he undertook as an artist, even when it came to humorous stunts. His disdain for fame was so great that for many years it was almost impossible to read his poetry, due to the lack of available editions.

His painting is subtly inspired by the prehispanic textiles and *quipus* that interested him in his youth and by the arts and beliefs of the indigenous peoples he studied devotedly during his time in Europe. But the "knots" that traverse his canvases, drawings, and objects are not mere archeological reconstructions or pastiches, but variations employing forms from an ancestral culture as a point of departure. These variations provided a vehicle for Eielson's imagination and revealed a unique sensibility resulting from a blend of his recondite mysticism, his extreme versatility in multiple subjects and disciplines, and his passion for beauty. Eielson was never bored. The life he lived proves that the title he chose for one of his books, *To Live Is a Masterpiece*, was true.

As a person, Eielson always kept something secret, an intimacy he preserved even beyond the reach of his closest friends. This mysterious depth intrigued and fascinated those who knew him and is a salient feature of his writing, sculpture, and paintings. Perhaps this depth will help ensure that his visual and poetic works endure. Though inseparable from the period in which it was created, Eielson's work deserves to live on and bear witness for future generations to the myths, dreams, miseries, and achievements pertaining to the world in which Eielson both suffered and enjoyed his life.

Florence, Italy, 2008

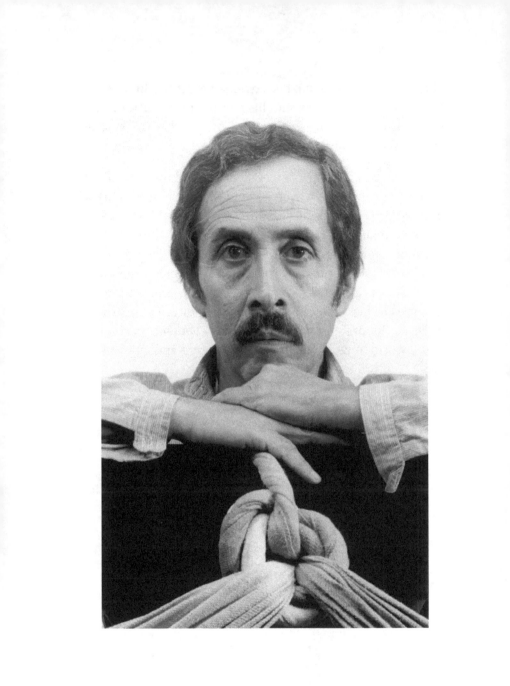

Et quae tanta fuit Romam tibi causa videndi?

VIRGIL

ELEGÍA BLASFEMA PARA LOS QUE VIVEN EN EL BARRIO DE
SAN PEDRO Y NO TIENEN QUÉ COMER

señores míos
por favor
traten de comprender
detrás de esa pared tan blanca
no hay nada
pero nada
lo cual no quiere decir
que no haya cielo
o no haya infierno
sería como confundir el sol
con un silbido
o con el propio cigarrillo
(no haber visto nunca el cielo
significa solamente
no tener dinero
ni para los anteojos)
pero que detrás de esa pared tan blanca
circule un animal tan fabuloso
arrastrando según dicen
siempre radiante
siempre enjoyado
un manto de cristal siempre encendido
y que su vivir sea tan brillante
que ni la vejez
ni la soledad
ni la muerte
amenacen su plumaje
no lo creo
ni puedo concebir tampoco
que además sea invisible

Blasphemous Elegy for Those Who Live in the Neighborhood of San Pedro and Have Nothing to Eat

my lords
please
try to understand
behind this white white wall
there is nothing
nothing at all
which doesn't mean
that there is no heaven
or that there is no hell
that would be like confusing the sun
with a whistle
or with your cigarette
(never having seen the sky
only means
not even having the money
for eyeglasses)
but I don't believe
that behind this white white wall
there paces such a fabulous animal
dragging so they say
always radiant
always bejeweled
a crystal blanket always aflame
or that its living is so brilliant
that neither old age
nor solitude
nor death
threaten its plumage
nor can i conceive
that it's invisible too

o demasiado parecido
al cielo azul
al árbol verde
al fruto rojo
al pan dorado
un animal tan milagroso
carecería de vientre
no tendría tantos hijos
negros   blancos   amarillos
que amanecen diariamente
con la cara ensangrentada
y los brazos amarrados
con la lengua acuchillada
y el estómago vacío
un animal así
no tendría el hocico sedoso de los vendedores de gracias
y ataúdes y estampas y souvenirs de instantes
perfectamente
olvidados bajo un cenicero o una postal de san pedro
una bestia semejante
tendría alas además
pero no alas de plumas encendidas
qué tontería
sino membranas divididas netamente
por la naturaleza
a izquierda y derecha
simétricamente dispuestas para volar un día
por sobre la pared tan blanca
por sobre el hambre y la guerra
o más humildemente
por sobre el resfriado y el cáncer
no señores míos
créanme realmente
detrás de esa pared tan blanca

or too similar
to the blue sky
to the green tree
to the red fruit
to golden bread
an animal so miraculous
would lack a womb
wouldn't have so many children
black   white   yellow
that wake daily
with faces bloodied
and arms tied
with tongues slashed
and stomachs empty
an animal like this
would not have a novelty peddlers' sleek snout   `
and coffins and stamps and souvenirs from moments
perfectly
forgotten beneath an ashtray or a postcard from san pedro
such a beast
would have wings too
but not wings with burning feathers
how dumb
rather membranes clearly parted
by nature
to the left and right
symmetrically available to one day fly
over the top of the white white wall
over the top of hunger and war
or more humbly
over the top of colds and cancer
no my lords
believe me truly
behind that white white wall

no hay nada
pero nada
una criatura tan perfecta además
no podría vivir encerrada
toda una eternidad
en un lugar tan hediondo
no podría vivir
alimentándose tan sólo
de su propio cuerpo luminoso
cómodamente tendido
en la gran pompa celeste
como si se tratara
de una espléndida ramera ya cansada
llena de mil hijos de mil padres olvidados bajo un cenicero
o una postal de san pedro

there's nothing
nothing at all
besides such a perfect creature
couldn't live enclosed
for an eternity
in such a stinking place
couldn't live
nourishing itself only
on its own luminous body
comfortably splayed across
the grand splendor of the heavens
as if it were
a gorgeous tired prostitute
full of the thousand children of a thousand parents
forgotten beneath an ashtray
or a postcard from san pedro

VALLE GIULIA

a giuseppe ungaretti

a dónde quiere llegar ese hom
bre con su bastón que
se quiebra siempre se quie
bra al doblar una esqui
na
extremidades de plomo ante escaleras
que surgen diariamente
de un huevo fragilísimo
y vuelven al huevo
fragilísimo
cabeza de reptil poeta
amarillo
exagerado de pájaro amarillo
que atraviesa el comedor y la cocina
o silba por las calles día y noche
pues tal es su alegría
que empieza a derramar el vino
en la vereda
a declamar sus versos
en el techo
indeseable reptil amarillo
(dicen los vecinos asustados)
extremidades de plomo cierto
no de pájaro
quién puede ser sino el fantoche
del amarillo mes de abril
en valle giulia
bastón inútil que se quie
bra en cada esqui
na
muy serenamente ya

VALLE GIULIA

to giuseppe ungaretti

where does that ma
n want to go with his cane that
breaks always bre
aks on turning the cor
ner
lead limbs before stairs
that rise daily
from so fragile an egg
and return to the egg
so fragile
reptile head poet
the exaggerated
yellow
of the yellow bird
that crosses the dining room and kitchen
or whistles through the streets day and night
such is his joy
that he begins to spill the wine
on the sidewalk
to spout his verses
from the roof
undesirable yellow reptile
(say the scared neighbors)
lead limbs true
not a bird's
who can it be but the braggart
of the yellow month of april
in valle giulia
useless cane that bre
aks on every cor
ner

su cuerpo
sube al cielo convertido
en un reptil alado que se aleja
en una pompa de jabón que no se quie
que no se quie
que no se quie
bra

very serenely now
his body
rises to the sky turned
into a winged reptile that floats away
on a soap bubble that doesn't bre
that doesn't bre
that doesn't bre
ak

Via della Croce

frecuentemente
cuando estoy sentado
en una silla
y estoy solo
y no he dormido
ni comido ni bebido
ni amado
tengo la impresión
de caer en un abismo
amarrado a mis vestidos
y a mi silla
y de irme muriendo suavemente
acariciando mis vestidos
y mi silla
tengo la impresión
de caer en un abismo
y de improviso asistir
a una remota fiesta
en el fondo de una estrella
y de bailar en ella
tiernamente
con mi silla

VIA DELLA CROCE

frequently
when i am seated
in a chair
and am alone
and haven't slept
or eaten or drunk
or loved
i have the sensation
of falling into an abyss
tied to my clothing
and to my chair
and of softly dying
caressing my clothing
and my chair
i have the sensation
of falling into an abyss
and unexpectedly attending
a faraway party
in the depths of a star
and of dancing at it
tenderly
with my chair

POEMA PARA LEER DE PIE EN EL AUTOBÚS ENTRE LA PUERTA FLAMINIA Y EL TRITONE

puedo escribir
así
de ti
contigo
sin ti
tal vez
silbando
como quien no
quiere nada
nada nada nada nada nada nada
o llorando
o comiendo
o bebiendo
o muerto de hambre
resfriado
estornudando
gritando
criatura
que no canto
no pido
no deseo
sino un poco
de alegría
muñeco de las causas
imposibles
monstruo que el rayo ha convertido
en una sonrisa
puedo escribir así
sobre ti
y sobre mí
y nada más

POEM TO READ WHILE STANDING ON THE BUS BETWEEN
THE FLAMINIA STOP AND TRITONE

i can write
like this
of you
with you
without you
perhaps
whistling
like someone who
wants nothing
nothing nothing nothing nothing nothing nothing
or crying
or eating
or drinking
or dying of hunger
sniffling
sneezing
yelling
sweetheart
i don't sing
don't ask
don't desire
anything but a bit
of joy
doll of lost
causes
monster that the lightning has turned
into a smile
i can write like this
about you
and about me
and nothing more

qué tristeza
tú y yo
y nada más
y las calles doradas
de roma
y tú y yo
y nada más
y qué más puede haber
de tú y yo
y los ojos celestes
de roma además
pero qué inútil
tanta luz
entre dos
qué tristeza
tú y yo
y nada más
qué tristeza
escribir y escribir y escribir y escribir
de los dos
hay que ver
prueben
qué harían ustedes
en situaciones tan horrendas
en una habitación tan oscura
sin puertas y sin ventanas
pero claveteada por dentro
sellada por fuera
completamente cubierta de flores perfumadas como los
crisantemos los nardos y otras flores semejantes
una especie de sarcófago en suma
y qué harían ustedes
qué harían
si tuvieran una pierna

what sadness
you and me
and nothing more
and the golden streets
of rome
and you and me
and nothing more
and what more can there be
of me and you
and the blue eyes
of rome too
but how useless
so much light
between the two
what sadness
to write and write and write and write
of the two
you have to see
try it out
what would you do
in such horrendous circumstances
in such a dark room
without doors and windows
but nailed shut from the inside
sealed from the outside
completely covered in perfumed flowers
chrysanthemums nards and other like flowers
a type of sarcophagus in short
and what would you do
what would you do
if you had a leg
in place of a nose
and walked with it
day and night along the tiber

en lugar de una nariz
y caminaran con ella
día y noche al pie del tíber
pidiendo limosna a las nubes
desenterrando objetos llameantes
buscando a dios entre las patas
de una mesa
qué harían
a ver
qué harían entonces
seres con rabo
que la sombra ha pisoteado
respondan temerosos
oh piadosos
maquinarias de rodillas
ante el gran dios fiat
si todo desapareciera bruscamente
por el ojo de la cerradura
del hotel ripetta
o ardieran vuestras propiedades
en un futuro silencio
de uranio
o llovieran carne y huesos
en el vaticano
escupieran pájaros los niños
cruzaran balas
deslumbrantes
flechas
de inusitado poder
afrodisíaco y purgante
y algo más
todavía
yo estúpido animal
avanzo siempre siempre

begging the clouds for alms
digging up flaming objects
seeking god among the legs
of a table
what would you do
let's hear
what would you do then
beings with a tail
crushed by shadow
respond fearful ones
oh pious ones
machinery of knees
before the great god fiat
if everything abruptly disappeared
through the eye of the keyhole
at the ripetta hotel
or your properties burned
in a future silence
of uranium
or it rained flesh and blood
over the vatican
children spat birds
dazzling
bullets crossed
arrows
of rare power
aphrodisiacal and purgative
and something else
still
i stupid animal
always always moving forward
until the final corners
where the sun urinates
the full moon urinates

sin embargo
avanzo siempre siempre
hasta los últimos rincones
donde se orina el sol
se orina la luna llena
se orinan los borrachos
vocifera la mierda
aúlla la soledad
criaturas que arrastráis
un solo
largo
llanto
no tengo nada
nada que ofreceros
ésta es la realidad
mi vida es humo
humo mi casa
y mis amigos
no reconozco
las dos huellas de mis pies
ni mis rodillas
en la arena
pero miro finalmente
el cielo arriba
el cielo abajo
arriba
abajo
arriba finalmente
fijamente
sin temor
ya no por el hueco
de la cerradura
por donde miraba entonces
¿recuerdas pobre jorge?

the drunks urinate
shit boasts
solitude howls
creatures dragging
one single
prolonged
wail
i have nothing
to offer you
this is reality
my life is smoke
smoke my house
and my friends
i don't recognize
my two footprints
or my knees
in the sand
but i finally see
the sky above
the sky below
above
below
above finally
fixedly
without fear
no longer through
the keyhole
i looked through before
remember poor jorge?
at the whore at the ripetta
hotel
thinking that
she too
was heavenly

a la puta del hotel
ripetta
creyendo que era celeste
ella también
magnitud ígnea
meteoro cuya caída
es el perfume
cuya memoria
es la memoria
de una joven en el trigo
y no era sino un hocico
pintado
dos bolsas de trapo
tres bolsas de trapo
seis bolsas de trapo
y un estómago sonoro
sonrío ahora ya
finalmente
he aquí mi oficio
pero cuánto me ha costado
he convertido en agua
mi paciencia
en pan
mi soledad
doy de comer
a los muros
de beber
a las sillas
me quema todo
y todo me congela
no sé leer
ni escribir
ni contar
y lo que es claro para todos

igneous magnitude
meteor whose fall
is the scent
whose memory
is the memory
of a young woman in the wheat
and wasn't anything but a spotted
snout
two bags of rags
three bags of rags
six bags of rags
and a growling stomach
now i smile
finally
here is my trade
but it's cost me so much
i have turned
my patience
into water
my solitude
into bread
i give food
to the walls
drink
to the chairs
everything burns me
and everything freezes me
i don't know how to read
or write
or count
and what is clear to all
is darkness to me
i'm useless
even for talking

para mí es tinieblas
no sirvo para nada
ni para conversar
conmigo mismo
ni para devorar
la televisión
o el cine
no sirvo para nada
no soy nada
esto lo sé
pero cuando me despierto
cosa que hago siempre
antes que los demás
las estaciones brillan
y cuando estoy dormido
es el invierno
generalmente además
soy más alto de día
que de noche
aunque alto no sea
(yo no sé por qué
mi madre hablaba siempre
de mi padre
como de un caballo
grande y silencioso
como un perro
o de un perro grande
y silencioso
como un caballo
la verdad es que mi padre
era tan alto
y encendido
que me era difícil mirarlo
y cuando lo miraba

to myself
or for devouring
television
or the cinema
i'm useless
i'm nothing
i know this
but when i wake up
something i always do
before everyone else
the seasons shine
and when i am sleeping
it is winter
generally also
i am taller by day
than by night
although i'm not tall
(i don't know why
my mother always spoke
of my father
like a
big silent
horse
like a dog
or like a dog big
and silent
like a horse
the truth is that my father
was so tall
and blazing
that it was difficult for me to look at him
and when I looked at him
the sun fell down my throat)
but it's useless

me caía el sol en la garganta)
pero de nada sirve
de nada sirve escribir
siempre sobre sí mismo
o de lo que no se tiene
o se recuerda solamente
o se desea solamente
yo no tengo nada
nada repito
nada que ofreceros
nada bueno sin duda
ni nada malo tampoco
nada en la mirada
nada en la garganta
nada entre los brazos
nada en los bolsillos
ni en el pensamiento
sino mi corazón sonando alto alto
entre las nubes
como un cañonazo

it's useless to always be
writing about oneself
or what one doesn't have
or just what one remembers
or just what one desires
i have nothing
i repeat nothing
nothing to offer you
nothing good no doubt
nor anything bad either
nothing in my gaze
nothing in my throat
nothing between my arms
nothing in my pockets
nor in my mind
but my heart ringing high high
among the clouds
like the boom of a cannon

Via Appia Antica

heme sin cabeza y sin calzado
esperando tu llegada
con una mano azul y otra amarilla
para ocultar mi tristeza
mientras la lluvia empieza
y un saxofón de plata suena y suena
en la via appia
un par de anteojos oscuros
y besarte siempre en los ojos
mientras se mueve el sol
de un día a otro
y tus vestidos vuelan incendiados
por la via appia
con mi corazón latiendo siempre
siempre siempre siempre siempre
un par de anteojos oscuros
y tal vez un saxofón
por la via appia

Via Appia Antica

here i am headless and shoeless
awaiting your arrival
with one hand blue and the other yellow
to hide my sadness
while the rain begins
and a silver saxophone wails and wails
on via appia
a pair of dark glasses
and to always kiss you on your eyes
while the sun moves
from one day to another
and your dresses fly ablaze
down via appia
with my heart always beating
always always always always
a pair of dark glasses
and perhaps a saxophone
down via appia

Azul ultramar

mediterráneo ayúdame
ayúdame ultramar
padre nuestro que estás en el agua
del tirreno
y del adriático gemelo
no me dejes vivir
tan sólo de carne y hueso
haz que despierte nuevamente
sin haber nunca dormido
haz que no llore nunca
haz que no muera nunca
haz que circule tu sonrisa
haz que no haya nada oscuro
nada amarillo
nada rojo
nada violeta ni verde
haz que amanezca nuevamente
esta ciudad que es tuya
y sin embargo es mía
esta ciudad que beso día y noche
como besaba lima en la niebla
y luego besé parís
y mañana besaré moscú
nueva york y tokio
londres y pekín
y enseguida besaré la luna
y más tarde marte
venus y saturno
y toda la vía láctea
hasta las últimas estrellas
mediterráneo ayúdame
ayúdame ultramar

OVERSEAS BLUE

mediterranean help me
help me overseas
our father who art in the water
of the tyrrhenian
and its twin adriatic
don't let me live
just as flesh and blood
make me wake back up
without ever having slept
make me never cry
make me never die
make your smile linger
make there be nothing dark
nothing yellow
nothing red
nothing violet or green
make this city that is yours
and nonetheless mine
wake back up
this city that i kiss day and night
like i kissed lima in the fog
and then i kissed paris
and tomorrow i'll kiss moscow
new york and tokyo
london and peking
and right away i'll kiss the moon
and later mars
venus and saturn
and all the milky way
till the last stars
mediterranean help me
help me overseas

lo vertiginoso
se apodera de mi cuerpo
resplandece entre mis brazos
baila con el sol en la azotea
y la luna en la cocina
la noche devastadora
es una máquina que brilla
una astronave de oro
una ecuación que avanza
avanza
avanza
y caen mil puertas de carne de hueso
y yo que corro corro corro
sigo corriendo todavía
y caen mil puertas más
tropiezo con una silla
huyo por las alcantarillas
salgo de los espejos
caigo ante columnas impalpables
y dolores de cabeza
me levanto
y caigo nuevamente
me levanto
y caigo nuevamente
entre las patas de los cerdos
finalmente
y lo vertiginoso es un muchacho
completamente inmóvil
una esfera solamente
una naranja quizás
todo en aras
de dulzuras que no existen
de nauseabundas criaturas
que gobiernan lo imposible

dizziness
takes control of my body
gleams in my arms
dances with the sun on the terraced roof
and the moon in the kitchen
the devastating night
is a shiny machine
a golden spaceship
an equation advancing
advancing
advancing
and a thousand doors of flesh of bone fall
and i who run run run
keep running still
and a thousand more doors fall
i stumble over a chair
i run through the sewers
i come out of the mirrors
i fall before impalpable columns
and headaches
i get up
and fall back down
i get up
and fall back down
between the pigs' hooves
finally
and the dizziness is a boy
completely still
just a sphere
perhaps an orange
everything for the sake
of sweetnesses that don't exist
of nauseating creatures
that govern the impossible

lo inesperado y lo inútil
ayúdame ultramar
ayúdame pez dorado
cae mi cuerpo de lo alto
de una cúpula sin vida
cae el sol y cae la luna
cae la norma
y ciudades y estatutos
caen las leyes
en racimos congelados
¿en dónde está mi doble
palpitante y escondido
mi corazón encogido
y su quejido?
¿en dónde está
en dónde está
mi corazón   mi corazón
tambores bajo el tíber
trompetas en el foro
mi corazón   mi corazón
mi corazón   mi saxofón
mi saxofón   mi corazón
mi coraxón   mi saxozón
en dónde está
en dónde está
el corazón
de esta ciudad que es tu cuerpo
y es el mío
nuestro cuerpo
y nuestro río
nuestra iglesia
y nuestro abismo?
esta ciudad con casas
con restaurantes

the unexpected and the useless
help me overseas
help me golden fish
my body falls from on high
from a lifeless cupola
the sun falls and the moon falls
the standard falls
and cities and statues
the laws fall
in frozen clusters
where is my double
throbbing and hidden
my shrunken heart
and its moan?
where is it
where is it
my heart   my heart
drums beneath the tiber
trumpets in the forum
my heart   my heart
my heart   my saxophone
my saxophone   my heart
my heartophone   my saxoheart
where is it
where is it
the heart
of this city which is your body
and is mine
our body
and our river
our church
and our abyss?
this city with houses
with restaurants

con automóviles
con fábricas y cinemas
teatros y cementerios
y escandalosos
avisos luminosos
para anunciar a dios con insistencia
con deslumbrantes criaturas
de papel policromado
que devoran coca-cola
bien helada
con espantosos remates
de vestidos usados
sexo y acción
heroísmo y pasión
technicolor por doquier
con elegantes
señores que sonríen y sonríen
y operarios que trabajan y trabajan
con miserables avenidas
que huelen a ropa sucia
y miserable ropa sucia
que huele a puro mármol
(tal y cual como tu cuerpo
criatura
fabuloso bajo el ruido de mil klaxons
y motores encendidos)

with automobiles
with factories and cinemas
theaters and cemeteries
and scandalous
illuminated signs
insistently announcing god
with dazzling creatures
made of polychromatic paper
that devour the coldest
coca-cola
with frightening sales
on used dresses
sex and action
heroism and passion
technicolor everywhere
with elegant
gentlemen who smile and smile
and machinists who labor and labor
with miserable avenues
that smell like dirty clothes
and miserable dirty clothes
that smell like pure marble
(just like your body
sweetheart
fabulous beneath the sound of a thousand horns
and running motors)

Via Veneto

me pregunto
si verdaderamente
tengo manos
si realmente poseo
una cabeza y dos pies
y no tan sólo guantes
y zapatos y sombrero
y por qué me siento
tan puro
más puro todavía
y más próximo a la muerte
cuando me quito los guantes
el sombrero y los zapatos
como si me quitara las manos
la cabeza y los pies

VIA VENETO

i ask myself
if i truly
have hands
if i truly possess
a head and two feet
and not just gloves
and shoes and a hat
and why i feel
so pure
even purer still
and closer to death
when i remove my gloves
my hat and my shoes
as if removing my hands
my head and my feet

Primavera en Villa Adriana

esta mañana de abril
las hojas verdes cubren
el corazón de paolo
que no puede caminar
ni decir una palabra
porque la vida pesa
esta mañana de abril
como un templo de papel
en el oxígeno puro
y si dijera una palabra
tan sólo una palabra
ardería el mundo entero

Spring in Villa Adriana

this april morning
the green leaves cover
paolo's heart
he can't walk
or say a word
because life is heavy
this april morning
like a temple of paper
in pure oxygen
and if he said a word
just a single word
the whole world would burn

CAMPIDOGLIO

usted no sabe cuánto pesa
un corazón solitario
hay noches en que la lana oscura
la lana tibia que me protege
llega hasta el cielo
y mientras duermo mientras respiro
mientras sollozo
se me derrama la leche hirviendo
sobre la cara
y entonces una máscara magnífica
con la sonrisa del rey de espadas
cubre mi llanto
y todo eso no es nada todavía
usted no me creerá
pero luchar luchar luchar
todas las noches con un tigre
hasta convertirlo en una magnolia
y despertarse
despertarse todavía y no sentirse
aún cansado y rehacer aún
raya por raya el mismo tigre odiado
sin olvidar los ojos los intestinos
ni la respiración hedionda
todo eso para mí
es mucho más fácil mucho más suave
créame usted
que arrastrar todos los días
el peso de un corazón desolado

CAMPIDOGLIO

you don't know how much
a solitary heart weighs
there are nights when the dark wool
the tepid wool that protects me
reaches to the sky
and while i sleep while i breathe
while i sob
boiling milk spills
down my face
and then a magnificent mask
with the king of spades' smile
hides my weeping
and all of that is nothing yet
you won't believe me
but fighting fighting fighting
every night with a tiger
till turning it into a magnolia
and waking up
still waking up and not feeling
tired yet and even recreating
stripe by stripe the same hated tiger
without forgetting its eyes its intestines
or its foul breath
all of that for me
is much easier much kinder
believe me
than having each day to drag along
the weight of a desolate heart

FORO ROMANO

todas las mañanas cuando me despierto
el sol arde fijo en el cielo
el café con leche humea en la cocina
yo le pregunto a quien me acompaña
¿cuántas horas he dormido?
pero nadie me responde

abro los ojos y los brazos buscando un apoyo
toco mi mesa de madera y la noche cae con violencia
un relámpago apaga la luz del sol
como la luz de una vela
vuelvo a preguntar
¿el café con leche de hace siglos humea aún en el polvo?
pero nadie me responde

en la oscuridad me levanto y lo bebo
pero compruebo que la leche está helada
y el café encendido yace como el petróleo
a varios kilómetros bajo tierra:
una silenciosa columna se desploma entre mis brazos
convertida en cenizas
bruscamente el sol vuelve a elevarse
y a declinar rápidamente
en una tempestad de hojas y pájaros rojizos
dentro de mi habitación el crepúsculo brilla un instante
con sus cuatro sillas de oro en las esquinas
trato de recordar mi infancia con las manos
dibujo árboles y pájaros en el aire como un idiota
silbo canciones de hace mil años
pero otra columna de cenizas se desploma entre mis brazos
y mis manos caen cubiertas de repentinas arrugas

ROMAN FORUM

every morning when i wake up
the sun seethes steady in the sky
the café con leche steams in the kitchen
i ask my companion
how many hours did i sleep?
but no one answers me

i open my eyes and my arms looking for support
i touch my wooden table and the night falls violently
a bolt of lightning blows out the light of the sun
like the light of a candle
i ask again
does the centuries-old café con leche still steam up from the dust?
but no one answers me

in the darkness i get up and drink it
but i realize that the milk is frozen
and the burning coffee rests like petroleum
several miles beneath the earth:
a silent column collapses in my arms
turned into ash
the sun brusquely rises again
and rapidly sets
in a storm of leaves and reddish birds
inside my bedroom the dusk shines for an instant
with its four golden chairs in the corners
i try to remember my childhood with my hands
i draw trees and birds in the air like an idiot
i whistle songs from a thousand years ago
but another column of ashes collapses in my arms
and my hands drop covered in sudden wrinkles

claramente ahora el agua del lavabo
me recuerda mis primeros baños en el río
vagos rumores desnudos perfumes viento
cerdos empapados bajo la sombra de los naranjos
¿mi memoria es quizás tan inmortal como tu cuerpo
cuando te desnudas ante mí
tú que no eres sino un pedazo de mármol
montaña de polvo
columna
reloj de ceniza
hueso sobre hueso que el tiempo avienta en mis ojos?
¿no recuerdo acaso las últimas horas de la noche
cuando te besaba enfurecido sobre mi catre de hierro
como si besara un cadáver?
yo le pregunto a quien me acompaña
amor mío velocísimo
¿cuánto tiempo ha pasado desde entonces
cuántas horas
cuántos siglos he dormido sin contemplarte?
pero nadie me responde

now the water in the sink clearly
reminds me of my first baths in the river
vague noises naked scents wind
mud-caked hogs beneath the orange trees' shade
might my memory be as immortal as your body
when you undress before me
you're nothing but a slab of marble
mountain of dust
column
clock of ash
bone on bone that time hurls in my eyes?
do i not perhaps remember the last hours of the night
when i kissed you furious on my iron cot
like i was kissing a cadaver?
i ask my companion
my fast fast love
how much time has passed since then
how many hours
how many centuries have I slept without contemplating you?
but no one answers me

TESTACCIO

oh no haber visto nunca
un cuchillo nunca una silla nunca
una estrella
dicen que en una noche
paolo transforma un cordero
en un suntuoso abanico
y que llorando luego
mira el cielo y amanece
luchando suavemente
con una vaca parturienta
todo eso está muy bien
pero por qué
por qué buscar la luz
en las entrañas de una oveja
y olvidar enseguida
el cuchillo en una silla
y no arrojar la silla
en una estrella
es verdad
que paolo vive solo en este mundo
apoyándose para ello en una mesa
construida con la misma madera
que todas las mesas
el pan la carne y el queso
naturalmente apartados y en la sombra
y que aún viviendo tan distantes
paolo y yo
ocupamos el lugar de una hormiga
y es verdad también que transcurren
días enteros boca arriba
mirando y mirando una turquesa
y que murmura

Testaccio

oh to never have seen
a knife never a chair never
a star
they say that in one night
paolo transforms a lamb
into a lavish fan
and then crying
looks at the sky and rises
gently fighting
with a cow in labor
all of this is very good
but why
why seek light
in the entrails of a sheep
and instantly forget
the knife on a chair
and not pitch the chair
on a star
it's true
that paolo lives alone in this world
hence leaning against a table
made with the same wood
as every table
the bread the meat the cheese
innately on their own and in the shade
and that even living so far apart
paolo and i
occupy the space of an ant
and it's also true that entire days
pass by belly up
staring and staring at a piece of turquoise
and that he murmurs

todo es inútil   todo es inútil
sí pero entonces ¿para qué cómo por qué
mirar la luna fijamente
entre las grandes nubes
de testaccio
y derramar temblando luego
sobre el cadáver de la oveja
el mismo balde de agua hirviendo
la misma mirada?

everything is useless   everything is useless
yes but then what for how why
stare at the moon intently
among the enormous clouds
of testaccio
and then trembling spill
the same bucket of boiling water
the same stare
over the sheep's cadaver?

PIAZZA DI SPAGNA

¿quién ha dicho que el cielo
no es sino un viejo tambor
completamente inútil
y sin sonido?
subamos por la escalinata
más suave del mundo
miremos hacia villa médicis
sin perder de vista
nuestra barca de mármol allá abajo
ni al capitán bernini
ni la pequeña isla
con sus tres palmeras africanas
a la diestra
y miremos el ocaso incomparable
que yo compararé sin embargo
a una trompeta
mejor
a todo un grupo de trompetas
mientras las nubes son violines
encendidos ciertamente
harpa el agua de las fuentes
contrabajo el viento fuerte
y los gorriones
flautas y caramillos
ninguna orquesta es concebible
sin un golpe de tambores
en el fondo
pero si el viejo cuero azul
resuena todavía
en trinidad del monte
ello se debe en gran parte
a un increíble sistema

PIAZZA DI SPAGNA

who has said that the sky
is nothing but an old drum
completely useless
and mute?
let's go up the softest
staircase in the world
let's look toward villa médicis
without losing sight of
our marble boat down below
nor of captain bernini
nor of the small island
with its three african palms
on its right side
and we will look at the incomparable sunset
that i will compare nonetheless
to a trumpet
better still
to an entire group of trumpets
while the clouds are violins
on fire certainly
harp the water from the fountains
upright bass the strong wind
and the sparrows
flutes and flageolets
no orchestra is conceivable
without the beat of drums
in the background
but if the old blue hide
still echoes
in trinidad del monte
that's due in large part
to an incredible system

de acústica divina
gracias al cual descubriremos
voces y melodías
que ya nadie escucha
volvamos para ello la cabeza
desde el último peldaño
de la augusta escalinata
justo en el mismo segmento
en donde la balaustrada maliciosa
suma ventitrés columnas
y cae a plomo bruscamente
desde un agudo obelisco
sobre la gran terraza
(por donde siempre pasa un niño
como un anillo sin dueño
el cabello rubio al viento
la voz completamente blanca)
y miremos a la izquierda
hacia abajo
hacia el ocaso nuevamente pero
más cerca de nosotros casi
a nuestro alcance apenas
a un tiro de escopeta
¿qué cosa vemos?
un segundo sol
más pequeño y luminoso
que el de siempre
y que se inclina lentamente
de nombre keats
un tercer sol diminuto como un niño
con el cabello rubio al viento
de nombre shelley
ambos ingleses y puros
niños poetas que la eternidad ha encerrado

of divine acoustics
thanks to which we will discover
voices and melodies
that no one hears anymore
let's turn our head for it
from the last step
of the august staircase
at precisely the same part
where the malicious balustrade
makes twenty-three columns
and plummets brusquely
from a sharp obelisk
over the grand terrace
(which a child always passes by
like a ring with no owner
blonde hair windblown
voice completely white)
and let's look to the left
downwards
back toward the sunset which
is almost closer to us
just out of our reach
a rifle shot away
what do we see?
a second sun
smaller and more luminous
than the same old one as always
and which slowly bows down
named keats
a third sun tiny like a child
blond hair windswept
named shelley
both english and pure
child poets that eternity has enclosed

en un mismo crepúsculo latino
juntos los dos y nunca divididos
ni por las mujeres
ni por la gloria
ni por la misma tierra elegida
dulces poetas de albión
¿duermen desnudos todavía
los estetas
en una alcoba de roma
perfecto dúo sin vida que aún murmura
una divina melodía
que ya nadie recuerda?

in the same latin dusk
the two of them together and never divided
not by women
not by glory
not by their shared chosen land
sweet albion poets
do the aesthetes
still sleep naked
in a bedroom in rome
perfect lifeless duo that still murmurs
a divine melody
that no one remembers anymore?

POEMA PARA DESTRUIR DE INMEDIATO SOBRE LA POESÍA
LA INFANCIA Y OTRAS METAMORFOSIS

damas y caballeros
las ventanas abiertas
ya no dan al cielo
como hace tanto tiempo
ni la pálida luna
que todos conocimos
alumbra el corazón
de los pastores
una pared muy alta
de cemento ciertamente
y una columna de humo
ocupan el lugar
que antes ocupaban
la pálida luna
leopardiana
y la retama
los burgueses dicen
es horrible
la municipalidad
no defiende nuestra luna
nuestro cielo
nuestras nubes
pero yo no comprendo
no comprendo francamente
cuántas veces
me despierto a medianoche
con los bolsillos llenos
de centellas
y es tan grande mi alegría
que se despiertan los vecinos
con un balde de agua fría

POEM TO DESTROY IMMEDIATELY ABOUT POETRY CHILDHOOD AND OTHER METAMORPHOSES

ladies and gentlemen
open windows
no longer face the sky
like so long ago
nor does the pale moon
that we all knew
light the heart
of shepherds
a very high wall
unquestionably made of cement
and a column of smoke
occupy the place
that the pale
leopardian
moon and the brambles
occupied before
the bourgeois say
it's horrible
the municipality
doesn't defend our moon
our sky
our clouds
but i don't understand
frankly i don't understand
how many times
i wake up at midnight
with my pockets full
of sparks
and my joy is so great
that the neighbors wake up
with a bucket of cold water

considerando un peligro
el mismo cielo encendido
y mi alegría
pero repito
no comprendo
quien fundó la luna
sobre roma
fabricó también el humo
el cemento y la mierda
perdonen la grosería
en cuanto al cielo
y a la luna
o la retama
¿cómo pueden reclamar
lo que nunca han conocido
sino en los pálidos versos
de un pálido poeta?
pero si las ventanas abiertas
ya no dan al cielo
ni a la pálida luna
estas puertas son en cambio
las misteriosas puertas
que dan a otras puertas
(recuerdo los veranos
de mi infancia en el perú
recuerdo una puerta de madera
un grupo de caballos empapados
y la luz de un lamparín
en el ocaso
recuerdo todavía
un viejo loro adormecido
en una silla
dos o tres caballos más
bajo la lluvia

considering
the same lit sky
and my joy
a danger
but i repeat
i don't understand
whoever set the moon
over rome
also manufactured the smoke
the cement and the shit
excuse the vulgarity
regarding the sky
and the moon
or the brambles
how can they claim
what they've only known
in the pale verse
of a pale poet?
but if unlatched windows
no longer open to the sky
nor the pale moon
these doors are instead
the mysterious doors
that open to other doors
(i remember the summers
of my childhood in peru
i remember a wooden door
a group of muddy horses
and the light of a lantern
in the dusk
i still remember
an old parrot dozing
on a chair
two or three more horses

y un plato de frijoles
en la mesa
pero no recuerdo bien
a qué hora
un torbellino de ceniza
me arrebató todo eso
y cayó la puerta de madera
cayó la luz del lamparín
y otra puerta de cristal
se abrió enseguida
hace millares de años
yo crucé esa puerta
fácilmente
pero en mi corazón
sucedieron varias cosas
que no entiendo
la pelota que yo arrojaba
al cielo gris de lima
la puerta que yo había creído
de madera
y hasta los mismos huesos
de mi madre enferma
se volvieron de turquesa
el mar brotó del caño roto
de la cocina
y desapareció por la ventana
del comedor
la luna ni la vi
y yo
qué tal idiota
me puse a llorar de inmediato
tras de un ramo
de retama
luego llegó una tía

beneath the rain
and a plate of beans
on the table
but i don't quite remember
at what moment
a whirlwind of ash
snatched all of that away from me
and the wooden door fell away
the light of the lantern fell away
and another glass door
suddenly opened
thousands of years ago
i crossed through that door
easily
but in my heart
several things happened
that i don't understand
the ball that i threw
into lima's gray sky
the door that i had thought was made
of wood
and even my sick mother's
bones themselves
turned turquoise
the sea sprang from the kitchen's
broken pipe
and disappeared through the dining room
window
i didn't even see the moon
and i
what an idiot
began immediately to cry
behind a bouquet
of brambles

con un rayo en la sortija
y una inmensa mantilla
llegaron luego un ruido
de cascabeles
y un vecino asustado
arrastrando una silla
sólo entonces
como lo hacía cada día
mi madre tomó asiento en ella
y murmuró
"el café con leche se enfría
criatura mía
¿qué estás esperando?")
damas y caballeros
podéis creerme ahora
amanecer es horrible
en estas condiciones
cada catre de hierro
es mi condena
cada silla de madera
una tortura
cada puerta que se cierra
una hecatombe
pero os repito
damas y caballeros
os repito
cuántas veces
me despierto a medianoche
con los bolsillos llenos
de centellas
y sin que nadie me descubra
como es ya mi costumbre
me pongo a llorar de inmediato
en la retama

later an aunt arrived
with a bolt of lightning
on the signet of her ring
and an immense shawl
then came the sound of
rattlesnakes
and a scared neighbor
dragging a chair
only then
as she did every day
did my mother sit in it
and murmur
"the café con leche is getting cold
my sweetheart
what are you waiting for?")
ladies and gentlemen
now you can believe me
waking up is horrible
in these conditions
each iron cot
is my sentence
each wooden chair
a torture
each door that closes
a catastrophe
but i repeat to you
ladies and gentlemen
how many times
do i wake up at midnight
with my pockets full
of sparks
without anyone noticing me
as is my habit now
i immediately begin to cry

estornudo sonrío
y hasta fumo un cigarrillo
entre las flores
y es tan grande mi alegría
que se despiertan los vecinos
con un balde de agua fría
puesto que a nadie se le ocurre
que fumar un cigarrillo
estornudar sonreír
o llorar entre las flores
sea sólo de alegría

in the brambles
i sneeze i smile
i even smoke a cigarette
among the flowers
and my joy is so great
that the neighbors wake up
with a bucket of cold water
since it occurs to no one
that smoking a cigarette
sneezing smiling
or crying among the flowers
might just be from joy

Albergo del Sole I

dime
¿tú no temes a la muerte
cuando te lavas los dientes
cuando sonríes
es posible que no llores
cuando respiras
no te duele el corazón
cuando amanece?

¿en dónde está tu cuerpo
cuando comes
hacia dónde vuela todo
cuando duermes
dejando en una silla
tan sólo una camisa
un pantalón encendido
y un callejón de ceniza
de la cocina a la nada?

ALBERGO DEL SOLE I

tell me
do you not fear death
when you brush your teeth
when you smile
is it possible that you don't cry
when you breathe
does your heart not hurt
when you wake up?

where is your body
when you eat
where does everything fly away to
when you sleep
leaving on a chair
just a shirt
a pair of pants on fire
and an alley of ash
between the kitchen and nothingness?

Albergo del Sole II

un día tú un día
abrirás esa puerta y me verás dormido
con una chispa azul en el perfil
y verás también mi corazón
y mi camisa de alas blancas
pidiendo auxilio en el balcón
y verás además
verás un catre de hierro
junto a una silla de paja
y a una mesa de madera
pero sobre todo
verás un trapo inmundo
en lugar de mi alegría
comprenderás entonces
cuánto te amaba
y por qué durante siglos
miraba sólo esa puerta y dibujaba
dibujaba y miraba esa puerta
y dibujaba nuevamente
con gran cuidado
comprenderás además
por qué todas las noches
sobre mi piel cansada
entre mil signos de oro
y tatuajes y arrugas majestuosas
me hacía llorar sobre todo
una cicatriz que decía:
yo te adoro yo te adoro yo te adoro

ALBERGO DEL SOLE II

one day you one day
will open that door and you will see me asleep
with a silhouette of blue sparks
and you will also see my heart
and my white-winged shirt
crying for help on the balcony
and you will also see
you will see an iron cot
next to a straw chair
and a wooden table
but in particular
you will see a filthy rag
instead of my joy
then you will understand
how much i loved you
and why for centuries
i only stared at that door and sketched
sketched and stared at that door
and sketched again
with great care
you will also understand
why every night
among the thousand gold marks
and tattoos and majestic wrinkles
on my tired skin
what made me cry the most
was a scar that said:
i adore you i adore you i adore you

JUNTO AL TÍBER LA PUTREFACCIÓN EMITE DESTELLOS GLORIOSOS

heme aquí juntando
palabras otra vez
palabras aún
versos dispuestos en fila
que anuncien brillantemente
con exquisita fluorescencia
el nauseabundo deceso
del amor
millares y millares
de palabras escritas
en un water-closet
mientras del cielo en llamas
de roma
cuelgan medias y calzoncillos
amarillos
cómo puedo yo escribir
y escribir tranquilamente
y a la sombra
de una cúpula impasible
de una estatua
que sonríe
y no salir gritando
por los barrios horrendos
de roma
y lamer las llagas de un borracho
desfigurarme la cara
con botellas rotas
y dormir luego en la acera
sobre los excrementos tibios
de una puta o un pordiosero

ALONGSIDE THE TIBER, PUTREFACTION TWINKLES GLORIOUSLY

here i am gathering
words again
words still
lines arranged single file
that brilliantly announce
the nauseating demise
of love
with exquisite fluorescence
thousands and thousands
of words written
in a water-closet
while yellow
briefs and stockings hang
from the flaming sky
of rome
how can i write
and write calmly
in the shade
of an impassive cupola
of a smiling
statue
and not wind up screaming
through the hideous neighborhoods
of rome
and lick a drunkard's sores
disfigure my face
with broken bottles
and then sleep on the sidewalk
in the warm excrement
of a streetwalker or a beggar

podría llenar cuartillas
y cuartillas aún peores
contar historias abyectas
hablar de cosas infames
que nunca he conocido
mi vergüenza es sólo un manto
de palabras
un delicado velo de oro
que me cubre diariamente
y sin piedad
pero si algún día
un instante junto al tíber
sin un ruido
ni un silbido
ni una nube
ni una mosca
al pie del río
con tan sólo
un cigarrillo
una cerilla
y una silla
en tanto estío
se levanta en mí un sollozo
¡oh maravilla!
semejante a una montaña
o a un mosquito que aparece
cada siglo en el cenit
aquel día
yo os lo juro
arrojaré al canasto
el universo entero
renacerá el amor
entre mis labios resecos

i could fill pages
and even worse pages
tell heinous stories
speak despicable things
that I have never known
my shame is just a cloak
of words
a delicate veil of gold
that covers me every day
without pity
but if one day
one instant by the tiber
without a sound
or a whistle
or a cloud
or even a fly
at the bank of the river
with just
a cigarette
a match
and a chair
in so much summer
a sob rises up inside me
oh wonder!
like a mountain
or a mosquito that appears
at the zenith of each century
that day
i swear to you
i will hurl the entire universe
into a wastebasket
love will be reborn
between my parched lips

y en estos versos dormidos
que ya no serán versos
sino balazos

and in these sleeping lines
that will no longer be lines
but gunshots

TRASTEVERE

cuando lo conocí paolo miraba
como es natural
una joven alta y luminosa
me dijo
dándome la mano de una orilla a otra
del tíber que tal vez soñaba
que no era cierto
que sin duda esa muchacha
no existía
y que la amistad
era tan sólo una palabra
luego me habló del pan
de cada día del vino rojo y de mujer e hijos
y de la inmensa pobreza
en que vivía
y viéndolo tan fuerte y abatido
yo pensaba
sería trabajo fácil para él
llevarse el día en un camión
subir al cielo en overall
desenterrar el huevo de la luz
y acariciarlo
noche tras noche hasta romperlo
y ver surgir a dios por fin
y nunca más partir al alba ni estrenar
con el primer café de cada día
la misma sonrisa carcomida

pero entretanto
la pobreza de paolo continuaba

Trastevere

when i met paolo he was staring
as is natural
at a tall, luminous young woman
he told me
offering me his hand from one side to the other
of the tiber that perhaps i was dreaming
that it wasn't true
that certainly that girl
did not exist
and that friendship
was just a word
later he spoke to me of daily
bread of red wine and of wife and children
and of the immense poverty
he lived in
and seeing him so strong and dispirited
i thought
it would be an easy job for him
to carry the day away in a truck
ascend to the sky in overalls
dig up the light's egg
and caress it
night after night until breaking it
and finally see god emerge
and never again leave at daybreak or debut
the same worm-eaten smile
with the first coffee of each day

but meanwhile
paolo's poverty continued

Llanto obligado (ante una fuente de Roma)

a s. salazar bondy
o de la entera amistad
roma, 1966

hay cosas que no comprendo
sino llorando
ríos de sangre por cierto
pero en sus manos un vaso de agua
y entre sus ojos un ruido atroz
de vidrios rotos
además caminaba ¿recuerdas?
caminaba todavía
cuando murió
es decir que se iba
naturalmente
que abandonaba
la mantequilla
que no volvía
más nunca
que su vestido
estaba vacío
que no veía
que no escuchaba
sino tambores
que conocía
que padecía
que describía
el desastre

Obligatory Cry (In Front of a Fountain in Rome)

to s. salazar bondy
or from our entire friendship
rome, 1966

there are things i don't comprehend
except when crying
rivers of blood by the way
but in his hands a glass of water
and between his eyes the atrocious sound
of broken glass
plus he was walking —remember?
he was still walking
when he died
which is to say that he went
naturally
that he abandoned
the butter
that he never came
back again
that his gown
was empty
that he didn't see
that he didn't hear
anything but drums
that he knew
that he endured
that he described
disaster

CAPILLA SIXTINA

hay personas
correctamente vestidas de gris
con camisa y corbata ciertamente
que a duras penas son personas
personas que se aventuran
con sus mil ojos cerrados
de escarabajos
bajo la cúpula divina
del florentino
personas que se arrodillan
ante sus pantorrillas
y sus inmensos traseros encendidos
antropófagos sin dientes
que ya no muerden sino admiran
sobre la pantalla atroz de la sixtina
en la carnicería final del buonarroti
el sangriento banquete de un magnate
o una película en colores
sobre hiroshima

Capilla Sixtina

there are people
rightly dressed in gray
most certainly in shirts and ties
that are barely people
people who venture
with their thousand closed
beetle eyes
beneath the florentine's
heavenly cupola
people who kneel
before his calves
and his giant flaming asses
toothless cannibals
that no longer bite but admire
a tycoon's bloody banquet
in buonarroti's final carnage
on the atrocious surface of the sistine
or a color film
about hiroshima

ESCULTURA DE PALABRAS PARA UNA PLAZA DE ROMA

Ce qui se montre est une vision de l'invisible.
ANAXAGORE DE CLAZOMENE

apareces
y desapareces
eres
y no eres
y eres nuevamente
eres todavía
blanco y negro que no cesa
y sólo existes
porque te amo
        te amo
        te amo
        te amo
        te amo
        te amo
escultura de palabras
escultura de palabras
escultura de palabras
escultura de palabras

apareces
y des   apareces
dejando un hueco encendido
entre la a y la s
un vacío entre los labios
una gota en la retina
¿qué cosa eres
verso sin fin
alineamiento fugaz
de vocales y consonantes

SCULPTURE OF WORDS FOR A PLAZA IN ROME

> Ce qui se montre est une vision de l'invisible.
> ANAXAGORE OF CLAZOMENE

you appear
and disappear
you are
and are not
and are again
and still are
ceaseless black and white
and you only exist
because i love you
    i love you
    i love you
    i love you
    i love you
    i love you
sculpture of words
sculpture of words
sculpture of words
sculpture of words

you appear
and dis   appear
leaving a burning hole
between the a and s
a gap between the lips
a drop on the retina
what are you
endless line
fleeting alignment
of vowels and consonants

qué cosa eres
macho y hembra confundidos
sol y luna en un instante?
no empieza nunca
no acaba nunca
lo luminoso y lo oscuro
no tienen barba ni senos
significa lo mismo
el caballo de marco aurelio
contro il logorio della vita moderna
cynar
a beautiful thing is a jewel forever
entre un abrir y cerrar de ojos
aparecen y desaparecen
el efebo de villa adriana
la decapitada de castelgandolfo
la dentadura de marilyn monroe
terreno baldío en donde juegan
niños verdosos y sin brazos
nauseabundas criaturas
arrastrando hasta la muerte
un manto ensangrentado
un centelleante juguete
que calcina
apareces y desapareces
¿no veré nunca
nunca tus mil ojos claros
con mis dos ojos negros nunca
tu cuerpo luminoso
entre mis brazos oscuros?
¿la luz hermafrodita que se asoma
entre los pliegues del profeta
es quizás
tu escultura de diamante

what are you
male and female confused
sun and moon in a single instant?
it never begins
it never ends
the luminous and the dark
have no beard or breasts
marcus aurelius's horse
means the same thing
contro il logorio della vita moderna
cynar
a beautiful thing is a jewel forever
the adonis of villa adriana
the decapitated woman of castel gandolfo
the teeth of marilyn monroe
appear and disappear
in the blink of an eye
empty lot where
greenish children with no arms
nauseating creatures
play dragging
a blood-drenched blanket
a sparkling toy
that scorches them
to their deaths
you appear and disappear
will i never see
your thousand clear eyes ever
with my two black eyes never
your luminous body
in my dark arms?
is the hermaphrodite light that peeks
between the prophet's pleats
perhaps

que nos llama
que nos llama
que nos llama
desde alfa de centauro?
apareces
y desapareces
eres y no eres
sino sonido   silencio   sonido
silencio nuevamente
sonido otra vez
hormigueo celeste
blanco y negro que no cesa
y sólo existes
porque te amo
          te amo
          te amo
          te amo
          te amo
          te amo

escultura de palabras
escultura de palabras
escultura de palabras
escultura de palabras

¿sabes tal vez que entre mis manos
las letras de tu nombre que contienen
el secreto de los astros
son la misma
miserable pelota de papel
que ahora arrojo en el canasto?

your diamond sculpture
that calls us
that calls us
that calls us
from alpha centauri?
you appear
and disappear
you are and aren't
if not sound   silence   sound
silence again
sound once more
celestial tingling
ceaseless black and white
and you only exist
because i love you
      i love you
      i love you
      I love you
      i love you
      i love you

sculpture of words
sculpture of words
sculpture of words
sculpture of words

do you perhaps know that in my hands
the letters of your name that contain
the secret of the stars
are the same
miserable ball of paper
that i now toss in the trashcan?

Martha L. Canfield

The artist and poet Jorge Eduardo Eielson (Lima, 1924 - Milan, 2006) was characterized by his love of novelty, his versatility, his kind but ironic gaze, his tireless playfulness, and lastly— this isn't a paradox—his luminous serenity. These qualities imbued his work, which was inseparable from his life, from his earliest creations up to his last, produced despite the immobility caused by his illness. Alvaro Mutis observed that through Eielson's works of visual art made of cloth, which he called *quipus* in reference to their pre-Columbian inspiration, "one enters a world of serenity and limpid beauty." This can be seen as much in the lyricism of his poetry as in the vigor and calm of his famous knotted fabrics.

Eielson's life and work were informed by his deep interest in Eastern philosophy, his search for harmony between East and West, and an attempt to reach a dissolution of the self. Throughout his trajectory, he proceeded steadily toward the contemplative stillness of Zen philosophy, of which he considered himself a fervent advocate. The brief compositions of *Naturaleza muerta* (Still life), written in Rome in 1958, suggest a form of reflection linked not to logic but rather to anti-logic or anti-mind, like the koans used in Zen practice by Buddhist monks.

> See the birds' silence
> Hear the flower's scent

Eielson's vision is associated on one hand with his continued pursuit of Zen thought, and on the other with his exploration of his historical and cultural roots, which soon led him to identify the knot associated with the *quipu* as central to his artistic and literary expression. Perhaps the clearest example of this is the delightful book *Nudos* (Knots), published in the Fundación César Manrique's Péñola Blanca collection in 2002. His partnership with Michele Mulas, a relationship that evolved into a spiritual and emotional union in constant growth over the course of the forty-something years they lived together, also contributed to the luminous evolution of this artist-poet.

The poetic subject of *Room in Rome* (1952), a tireless pilgrim on the streets of the Eternal City, seeks something he knows he cannot find, thus embodying the distressing bewilderment of our age. He also knows that while the object of his longing is transcendent, the place where it might be found is not; it may in fact be humble and unexpected. In this way, he expresses another fundamental Zen Buddhist teaching:

> and what would you do
> what would you do
> if you had a leg
> in place of a nose
> and walked with it
> day and night [...]
> seeking god among the legs
> of a table
> [...]

In *Room in Rome*, poetry emerges from the intense drama of daily life in the city. Here, we see the poetic subject battle poverty, loneliness, and isolation, but most of all the masks imposed by society, which destroy the integrity of the body—the vehicle and form of the soul. In this struggle, he moves toward a revelatory vision of the light at the center of the labyrinth. The same battle would appear in the series of poems later collected under the title *Noche oscura del cuerpo* (Dark night of the body), evoking Eielson's beloved St. John of the Cross.

From the poems of *Room in Rome*, written in the Italian city Eielson loved most, there also emerges a testimony of the lacerating contrast between Rome's great past, the magnificence of its ruins, and the poverty of the post-war capital; between the suggestive beauty—for example—of the Via Appia Antica, or the new riches displayed on Via Veneto, and the inner decay of the individual, "headless and shoeless," dreaming of easing his loneliness on Via della Croce with a dramatic dance with his own unpredictable, anthropomorphized chair.

Eielson's long, productive career can be divided into periods using geographical criteria. His early Lima phase corresponds to his assimilation of the neo-baroque, *conceptismo*, and the grotesque of the Spanish masters, and encompasses the collections *Moradas y visiones del amor entero* (Dwellings and visions of love in its entirety), *Cuatro parábolas del amor divino* (Four parables of divine love), *Canción y muerte de Rolando* (Song and death of Roland), *Reinos* (Kingdoms), *Antigone, Ajax en el infierno* (Ajax in hell), *En la Mancha* (In La Mancha), *El circo* (The circus), *Bacanal* (Bacchanal), and *Doble diamante* (Double diamond), written between 1942 and 1947. *Primera muerte de María* (The first death of María), written in Paris in 1949, but still showing the influence of his training in Lima, can also be said to belong to this period. In the experimental parenthesis that corresponds to *Tema y variaciones* (Theme and variations), written in Geneva in 1950, we see a split between the poetic self and the word, the latter becoming a purely sonic and graphic element. A second phase corresponding to Eielson's time in Rome is followed by the second parenthesis of the narrative poem *Ptyx* (Paris, 1980), with which he breaks his long poetic silence. A third and final phase in Milan lasts from the middle of the 1990s until the poet's death, and is characterized by the evocative, celebratory high lyricism of *Sin título* (Untitled), *Celebración* (Celebration), *Canto visible* (Visible song), and *Del absoluto amor* (On absolute love), published between 2000 and 2005.

Alongside his other Roman collection, *Noche oscura del cuerpo*, critics consider *Room in Rome* to be Eielson's masterpiece. The collection displays its author's rare ability to "knot" together past and present, tradition and novelty, the anguish of modern life and the resplendence of another, serene existence within reach. The author lived for a period at the Chelsea Hotel in New York, an experience that was crucial to his avant-garde orientation. Eielson would be happy to know that his Roman poems have come to life again in English and can now be read in the language spoken by his paternal family.

Florence, January 18, 2017

ABOUT THE TRANSLATOR

David Shook is a poet, translator, and editor who has translated over ten books from Spanish and Isthmus Zapotec, including work by Mario Bellatin, Kyn Taniya, and Víctor Terán. His writing has appeared in the *Guardian,* the *Los Angeles Review of Books,* and *Poetry,* among many other publications.

Previous page
BANDIERE (detail), 2002
Jorge Eduardo Eielson
Photograph by Karina Valcárcel

ABOUT THE AUTHOR

Jorge Eduardo Eielson was born in Lima on April 13, 1924 to a Peruvian mother and a Swedish father. After attending several different schools, at the end of his secondary studies he met the writer and anthropologist José María Arguedas, who introduced him to Lima's artistic and literary circles, and to a wealth of knowledge about the ancient civilizations of Peru. Three years later, at the age of 21, he won the National Poetry Award. He went on to receive the National Drama Award in 1948, the same year that the prestigious Lima Gallery hosted a well received exhibition of his visual art. In 1951, he traveled to Italy for a summer vacation and decided to settle in Rome, where he met his life partner, Michele Mulas. During this period he wrote his masterpiece *Habitación en Roma* (Room in Rome), and the two novels *El cuerpo de Giulia-No* (The body of Giulia-No) and *Primera muerte de María* (The first death of María). In the late 1950s, he began to texturize his works on canvas with organic materials such as earth, sand, and clay. This eventually led to his depiction of human forms using textiles, and in 1963 he began work on what would become his first *quipu*, reinventing this ancient Andean form with fabrics in brilliant colors, knotted and tied on canvas. Eielson's *quipus* were exhibited to wide acclaim at the 1964 Venice Biennale. In the mid-1970s, he returned to Peru to study pre-Columbian art more deeply; during this period, the Instituto Nacional de Cultura (National Institute of Culture) published the bulk of his poetry under the title *Poesía escrita* (Written poetry). Later in that decade, he moved to Milan, where he would spend the rest of his life writing, studying Zen, and producing his art, which was exhibited around the world. After the death of his partner in 2002, Eielson's own health deteriorated significantly, though his life was brightened by the discovery of several relatives previously unknown to him, including his sister Olivia. The poet died on March 8, 2006, and his ashes were laid to rest beside his partner's in the small cemetery in Bari Sardo.

C O N

T E N T S

CPSIA information can be obtained
at www.ICGtesting.com
Printed in the USA
FSHW011018270919